The Cop and the Anthem

*A Witty Holiday Tale of Hope,
Homelessness & Serendipity on
New York's Streets*

A Modern Translation
Adapted for the Contemporary Reader

O. Henry

Translated by Tim Zengerink

Table of Contents

Preface
Message to the Reader

Rebuilding the Greatest Library in Human History

Thousands of years ago, the Library of Alexandria was the heart of global knowledge — a sanctuary where the wisdom of every known civilization was gathered and shared freely.

And then, it was lost.

Now, we're rebuilding it — and you are invited to join us.

At the Library of Alexandria, we've set out to make every book available to every person on Earth — not just in print, but in every language, every format, and for every reader.

Here's how we do it:

- **Deluxe Print Editions at True Printing Cost** - Order any book as a high-quality paperback, elegant hardcover, or stunning boxset — and only pay what it costs to print. No markups. No middlemen.
- **Unlimited Access to the Greatest Works** - Enjoy thousands of timeless classics — from Plato to Shakespeare to Tolstoy — in beautiful, modern eBook and audiobook editions. Read and listen without limits — for every reader, everywhere.
- **Modern Translations for Every Language & Dialect** - We're reimagining the classics in clear, accessible language — and translating them into every dialect imaginable. Everyone deserves to understand humanity's greatest ideas.

When you visit **LibraryofAlexandria.com**, you're not just accessing books — you're joining a global movement to restore, preserve, and share the wisdom of civilization.

Join us today at LibraryofAlexandria.com

Together, we'll ensure the light of human wisdom never fades again.

With gratitude,

The Modern Library of Alexandria Team

Visit:
www.libraryofalexandria.com
Or scan the code below:

Introduction

O. Henry's Art of Irony and Compassion

O. Henry's *The Cop and the Anthem* stands as one of the most beloved short stories in American literature, not only for its trademark twist ending but also for its profound humanity and sharp social commentary. First published in *The New York World* newspaper on December 21, 1904, the story is quintessentially O. Henry—brimming with wit, irony, and a heartfelt understanding of people who live on the margins of society. Unlike conventional holiday tales that are drenched in sentimentality, this narrative approaches the theme of hope and redemption from an unexpected angle, using humor and misadventure to highlight the struggles of homelessness, the allure of second chances, and the unpredictable hand of fate.

The story centers on Soapy, a homeless man living on the streets of New York City. As winter approaches, Soapy devises a peculiar plan for survival: he wishes to be arrested and sent to Blackwell's Island, a prison where he can spend the cold months with food, shelter, and warmth. Rather than seeking charity or honest work, Soapy believes that jail is his best option—a testament both to his cynicism and to the harsh realities faced by those who lack stable housing. Over the course of the story, Soapy makes a series of increasingly desperate and comical attempts to get himself arrested. He tries everything from dining at an expensive restaurant without paying to throwing a stone through a shop window, yet each plan fails in absurd and ironic ways. It is only when Soapy, in a moment of unexpected inspiration, resolves to reform his life that he is finally arrested—not for his earlier antics, but for loitering near a church while listening to an uplifting anthem.

This final twist is vintage O. Henry: just as Soapy decides to turn his life around, fate intervenes with cruel and humorous irony, ensuring that his path is determined not by his intentions but by the random workings of chance. Through this story, O. Henry captures the fragility of human aspirations, particularly for those living on society's edges, while also crafting a narrative that is both deeply moving and delightfully entertaining.

What sets *The Cop and the Anthem* apart is its seamless blend of humor and poignancy. While Soapy's antics are undeniably comical—his failed schemes to provoke the police are a masterclass in situational irony—they also underscore the desperation of a man who feels trapped by circumstances and societal indifference. In O. Henry's hands, Soapy is not merely a caricature of a down-and-out vagrant; he is a fully realized character whose wit, cunning, and self-awareness make him sympathetic and even admirable in his resilience. His misadventures offer not just laughter but also a window into the complexities of poverty, pride, and the human longing for dignity.

The story's holiday setting adds another layer of meaning. Like Charles Dickens's *A Christmas Carol*, *The Cop and the Anthem is*, at its core, a story about transformation and hope. Yet O. Henry delivers this message in his own unique style—eschewing sentimentality in favor of sharp wit and a playful narrative structure. The anthem that inspires Soapy to rethink his life functions as a symbol of redemption and the possibility of a fresh start, but the twist ending reminds us that real change often comes not in dramatic epiphanies but through small, sustained efforts—

and that life's unpredictability can derail even the best intentions.

The humor and irony of this tale are further heightened by O. Henry's vivid portrayal of early 20th-century New York City. The bustling streets, the contrast between wealth and poverty, and the indifferent, fast-paced urban life serve as a backdrop for Soapy's personal struggles. New York, for O. Henry, is not merely a setting but a character in itself—a place of opportunity and misfortune, of anonymous crowds and fleeting moments of grace. Through Soapy's wanderings, the story paints a portrait of a city that is both harsh and vibrant, a place where dreams are forged and dashed in equal measure.

Understanding O. Henry's background helps illuminate the richness of this narrative. Born William Sydney Porter in 1862, O. Henry experienced many hardships in his own life, including financial difficulties, imprisonment, and a restless search for stability. These experiences imbued his writing with a deep empathy for people who struggle against adversity. His stories frequently focus on ordinary individuals—often those on the fringes of society—who face extraordinary situations with humor, resourcefulness, and a touch of luck (or misfortune). *The Cop and the Anthem* is a perfect example of this approach, blending comic misadventures with a poignant exploration of human resilience.

For the modern reader, the story offers both entertainment and insight. On one hand, it is a tightly plotted, humorous tale that can be enjoyed simply for its clever twists and engaging narrative voice. On the other hand, it invites deeper reflection on issues that remain relevant today: homelessness, social inequality, and the human yearning for purpose and belonging. Soapy's character resonates because he embodies both the struggles and the small victories of those who live without the security that many take for granted. His attempts to control his destiny—however misguided—reflect a universal desire for stability and meaning in a world that often seems indifferent.

As you approach *The Cop and the Anthem*, it is helpful to pay attention to O. Henry's masterful use of language. His prose is brisk, witty, and filled with colorful details that bring the city and its characters to life. The narrative voice, which combines humor with a subtle undercurrent of empathy, draws readers into Soapy's world, making them both laugh at his misadventures and root for his success. The story's pacing is another key strength; each of Soapy's failed attempts to get arrested adds to the comedic tension, building toward the final, unexpected resolution.

Moreover, O. Henry's trademark twist ending is not merely a gimmick but an integral part of the story's thematic structure. The irony of Soapy's arrest—coming at the very moment when he chooses to change—serves as a powerful reminder of life's unpredictability and the challenges of self-reinvention. This twist also invites readers to consider the broader social forces at play. Why is Soapy's only path to shelter and warmth through imprisonment? What does this say about society's treatment of the poor and the homeless? These questions, though posed with humor, give the story a depth and resonance that elevates it beyond mere entertainment.

Hope, Redemption, and the Human Spirit

At its heart, *The Cop and the Anthem* is a story about hope—hope that arises in unexpected places and moments. Soapy, despite his rough exterior and cynical outlook, is ultimately moved by the sound of music emanating from a church. This brief encounter with beauty and transcendence stirs something deep within him, reminding readers that even in the darkest circumstances, there is always the possibility of renewal. The anthem functions as both a literal and symbolic call to a higher purpose, suggesting that art, music, and spirituality can awaken the better angels of our nature.

Yet O. Henry, ever the realist and humorist, tempers this message of hope with a dose of irony. The fact that Soapy's newfound determination is immediately thwarted by his arrest underscores the difficulty of breaking free from one's circumstances, especially when society offers few pathways for those on the margins. This tension between hope and harsh reality is a hallmark of O. Henry's work. While he delights in crafting clever twists, his stories often reveal a deep compassion for the struggles of ordinary people.

One of the reasons *The Cop and the Anthem* has endured for more than a century is its universality. The themes of resilience, second chances, and the search for dignity are as relevant today as they were in O. Henry's time. Homelessness remains a pressing social issue, and Soapy's plight continues to resonate with readers who understand the precariousness of life without a safety net. By presenting these themes through humor and irony, O. Henry invites readers to engage with serious issues in a way that is both accessible and thought-provoking.

Another enduring aspect of this story is its characterization. Soapy is a memorable and complex protagonist, one who defies easy categorization. He is both a trickster and a dreamer, a man who navigates the harsh realities of the streets with cunning but who is also capable of moments of profound self-reflection. His failed attempts to get arrested—whether by causing disturbances, dining without paying, or attempting to harass women—are not just comic episodes but glimpses into his resourcefulness and his frustration with a society that seems to have no place for him. Readers cannot help but sympathize with Soapy, even as they laugh at his misadventures.

O. Henry's narrative also explores the relationship between individual choice and societal constraints. While Soapy's plans are often misguided, they stem from a rational assessment of his limited options. In a world where poverty is criminalized and the social safety net is minimal, jail becomes, paradoxically, a refuge. This irony—where punishment is sought as a form of protection—adds a layer of social critique to the story, making it not only entertaining but also subtly political.

Finally, *The Cop and the Anthem* reminds us of the power of small moments. Soapy's transformation is sparked not by a grand event but by the simple beauty of music drifting from a church. This moment of grace, however fleeting, highlights O. Henry's belief in the redemptive potential of everyday experiences. It is a reminder that even in the midst of hardship, there are moments of inspiration that can change the course of a life—if only for an instant.

The Cop and The Anthem

On his bench in Madison Square, Soapy shifted restlessly. When wild geese call out high in the night sky, and when women without expensive fur coats become gentle with their husbands, and when Soapy fidgets uncomfortably on his park bench, you can be sure that winter is approaching.

A dead leaf dropped onto Soapy's lap. This was Jack Frost's calling card. Jack treats the regular residents of Madison Square kindly and gives them fair notice of his yearly visit. At the intersection of four streets, he passes his card to the North Wind, the servant of the great mansion of All Outdoors, so that those who live there can prepare themselves.

Soapy realized that the time had come for him to figure out on his own how to prepare for the harsh winter ahead. So he shifted restlessly on his bench.

Soapy's winter plans weren't particularly grand. He didn't dream of Mediterranean cruises or drowsy Southern skies floating over the Bay of Naples. What his soul longed for was three months on the Island. Three months of guaranteed meals and shelter with pleasant company, protected from the harsh north wind and police officers, struck Soapy as the perfect arrangement.

For years, the welcoming Blackwell's had served as his winter home. Just as his wealthier fellow New Yorkers purchased their tickets to Palm Beach and the Riviera each winter, Soapy had made his modest preparations for his yearly journey to the Island. And now the time had arrived. The night before, three Sunday newspapers tucked under his coat, around his ankles, and across his lap had failed to keep out the cold as he slept on his bench near the bubbling fountain in the old square. So the Island appeared large and perfectly timed in Soapy's thoughts. He looked down on the arrangements made in the name of charity for the city's poor. In Soapy's view, the Law treated people more kindly than charitable organizations. There was an endless cycle of institutions, both government-run and charitable, where he could go and receive shelter and food that matched a simple way of living. But for someone with Soapy's proud nature, charitable gifts came with strings attached. If you didn't pay with money, you had to pay with damaged pride for every benefit you received from charitable hands. Just as Caesar had his Brutus, every charitable bed demanded the price of a bath, every loaf of bread required payment through private and personal questioning. Therefore, it was better to be a guest of the law, which, though it operated by strict rules, didn't interfere too much with a gentleman's personal business.

Soapy had made up his mind to go to the Island, so he immediately began working toward achieving his goal. There were numerous simple methods to accomplish this. The most enjoyable approach would be to eat an extravagant meal at an upscale restaurant, then announce he couldn't pay the bill and be peacefully turned over to a police officer without causing a scene. A cooperative judge would handle everything else.

Soapy got up from his bench and walked out of the square, crossing the flat expanse of asphalt where Broadway and Fifth Avenue meet. He turned up Broadway and stopped at a sparkling café, where the finest wines, silks, and people gathered together every night.

Soapy felt completely confident in his appearance from the bottom button of his vest all the way up. He was clean-shaven, his coat looked respectable, and his crisp black pre-tied necktie had been given to him by a lady missionary on Thanksgiving Day. If he could make it to a table in the restaurant without arousing suspicion, he would succeed. The part of him visible above the table wouldn't raise any questions in the waiter's mind. A roasted mallard duck, Soapy thought, would be perfect—along with a bottle of Chablis, followed by Camembert cheese, a small cup of coffee, and a cigar. One dollar for the cigar would be sufficient. The total bill wouldn't be high enough to provoke any extreme act of retaliation from the restaurant management, yet the meal would leave him satisfied and content for his trip to his winter shelter.

But when Soapy stepped through the restaurant door, the head waiter immediately noticed his worn-out pants and shabby shoes. Firm and efficient hands spun him around and quickly escorted him back to the sidewalk in silence, preventing the disgraceful destiny that threatened the duck.

Soapy turned away from Broadway. It appeared that his path to the desired island wouldn't be a pleasurable one. He needed to think of some other way to enter that place of waiting.

At the corner of Sixth Avenue, electric lights and cleverly arranged merchandise behind plate glass made a store window stand out. Soapy picked up a cobblestone and hurled it through the glass. People came running around the corner, with a police officer in front. Soapy remained motionless, keeping his hands in his pockets, and grinned when he saw the brass buttons.

"Where's the man who did that?" the officer asked excitedly.

"Don't you think I might have had something to do with it?" said Soapy with a touch of sarcasm, though in a friendly way, like someone welcoming good luck.

The police officer's mind wouldn't even consider Soapy as a suspect. People who break windows don't stick around to chat with law enforcement. They run away. The officer spotted a man halfway down the block running to catch a streetcar. With his club drawn, he joined the chase. Soapy, feeling disgusted, wandered along slowly, having failed twice now.

Across the street stood a simple restaurant with no fancy ambitions. It served people who were very hungry but didn't have much money to spend. The dishes and air inside were heavy and thick, while the soup and table linens were disappointingly thin. Soapy walked into this establishment wearing his worn-out shoes and shabby pants, and nobody questioned his presence. He took a seat at a table and ate his way through beefsteak, pancakes, doughnuts, and pie. When he finished, he revealed to the waiter that he didn't have even the smallest amount of money on him.

"Now, get busy and call a cop," said Soapy. "And don't keep a gentleman waiting."

"You're not getting any coffee," said the waiter, with a voice as smooth as butter and an eye like the cherry in a Manhattan cocktail. "Hey, Con!"

On the hard pavement, two waiters threw Soapy down, landing him squarely on his left ear. He got up slowly, unfolding himself piece by piece like a carpenter's measuring stick, and brushed the dirt off his clothing. Getting arrested now felt like nothing more than a pleasant fantasy. The Island seemed incredibly distant. A police officer standing in front of a pharmacy two storefronts away chuckled and continued walking down the street.

Soapy walked five blocks before he felt brave enough to try getting arrested again. This time the chance seemed like what he foolishly called a sure thing. A young woman with a modest and attractive appearance stood in front of a store window, looking with lively interest at the display of shaving mugs and inkwells, while just two yards away from the window a large, stern-looking policeman leaned against a fire hydrant.

Soapy planned to take on the role of a despicable and hated street harasser. The refined and elegant appearance of his target and the nearby presence of a dutiful police officer encouraged him to believe that he would soon feel the satisfying official grip on his arm that would guarantee his winter lodging on the secure little island.

Soapy adjusted the lady missionary's store-bought tie, pulled his worn cuffs out into view, tilted his hat at a rakish angle and moved toward the young woman. He flirted with her, suddenly started coughing and clearing his throat, smiled, grinned and boldly went through the shameless and despicable routine of a street harasser. Out of the corner of his eye, Soapy noticed that the police officer was watching him intently. The young woman stepped away a few paces and once again focused her complete attention on the shaving mugs. Soapy followed her, confidently moving to her side, tipped his hat and said:

"Hey there, Bedelia! Don't you want to come and play in my yard?"

The police officer was still watching. The harassed young woman only needed to signal with her finger and Soapy would be practically on his way to his island refuge. He could already imagine feeling the comfortable warmth of the police station. The young woman turned toward him and, reaching out her hand, grabbed Soapy's coat sleeve.

"Of course, Mike," she said happily, "if you'll buy me a beer. I would have talked to you earlier, but the police officer was keeping an eye on things."

With the young woman clinging to him like ivy to an oak tree, Soapy walked past the police officer, overwhelmed by despair. He appeared destined to remain free.

At the next corner he broke away from his companion and ran. He stopped in the neighborhood where at night you find the brightest streets, hearts, promises and song lyrics. Women wearing fur coats and men in heavy overcoats moved cheerfully through the cold winter air. A sudden fear gripped Soapy that some terrible spell had made him impossible to arrest. This thought brought with it a touch of panic, and when he encountered another police officer standing proudly in front of a magnificent theater, he grasped at the immediate opportunity of "disorderly conduct."

On the sidewalk, Soapy started shouting drunken nonsense at the top of his raspy voice. He danced, howled, ranted, and generally disrupted the peace.

The police officer spun his nightstick, turned his back to Soapy and made a comment to a passerby.

"'It's one of those Yale students celebrating the shutout they gave to Hartford College. They're noisy, but harmless. We have instructions to leave them alone."

Dejected, Soapy stopped his futile commotion. Would a police officer never arrest him? In his imagination, the jail seemed like an impossible paradise. He fastened his threadbare coat against the cold wind.

In a cigar shop, he spotted a well-dressed gentleman lighting his cigar at a hanging lamp. The man had placed his silk umbrella near the entrance when he came in. Soapy walked inside, grabbed the umbrella, and strolled away with it at a leisurely pace. The man who had been lighting his cigar quickly followed after him.

"My umbrella," he said sternly.

"Oh, really?" Soapy scoffed, making his petty theft even more insulting. "Well, why don't you call a police officer? I stole it. Your umbrella! Why don't you call a cop? There's one standing right on the corner."

The man with the umbrella began walking more slowly. Soapy did the same, sensing that his luck was about to turn bad once again. The police officer watched both men with curiosity.

"Of course," said the umbrella man—"that is—well, you know how these mistakes happen—I—if it's your umbrella I hope you'll forgive me—I picked it up this morning in a restaurant—If you recognize it as yours, well—I hope you'll—"

"Of course it's mine," said Soapy, viciously.

The former umbrella salesman backed away. The police officer rushed to help a tall blonde woman wearing an opera cloak cross the street, even though a streetcar was still two blocks away.

Soapy walked east down a street torn up by construction work. He angrily threw the umbrella into a construction pit. He grumbled about the police officers who wore helmets and carried nightsticks. Since he wanted to get arrested by them, they seemed to treat him like royalty who could do nothing wrong.

Eventually, Soapy arrived at one of the eastern avenues where the sparkle and commotion were only dim. He turned his face down this street toward Madison Square, because the instinct to return home persists even when home is just a park bench.

But on an unusually quiet corner, Soapy stopped walking. There stood an old church, charming and sprawling with decorative gables. Through one purple-tinted window, a gentle light shone, where the organist was likely lingering at the keyboard, practicing to perfect the upcoming Sunday hymn. Beautiful music floated out to Soapy's ears, capturing his attention and holding him motionless against the ornate iron fence.

The moon hung overhead, bright and peaceful; there were few cars and people walking by; sparrows chirped drowsily under the roof edges—for a moment the scene could have been a rural cemetery. And the hymn that the organ player performed held Soapy firmly against the iron fence, because he had known it well back when his life included things like mothers and roses and dreams and friends and pure thoughts and clean collars.

Soapy's open state of mind combined with the atmosphere surrounding the old church created a sudden and remarkable transformation in his spirit. He saw with immediate shock the depths to which he had fallen, the shameful days, worthless longings, crushed dreams, damaged abilities and dishonorable motivations that comprised his life.

His heart immediately responded with excitement to this new feeling. A sudden and powerful urge drove him to fight against his hopeless situation. He would lift himself out of this mess; he would become a real man again; he would overcome the evil that had taken control of him. There was still time; he was still relatively young; he would bring back his old passionate dreams and chase them without giving up. Those serious but beautiful organ sounds had started a revolution inside him. Tomorrow he would go into the busy downtown area and find work. A fur importer had once offered him a job as a driver. He would find that man tomorrow and ask for the position. He would become someone important in the world. He would—

Soapy felt someone place a hand on his arm. He quickly turned to see the wide face of a police officer looking at him.

"What are you doing here?" asked the officer.

"Nothing," said Soapy.

"Then come along," said the policeman.

"Three months on the Island," the Magistrate announced in the Police Court the following morning.

An Adjustment of Nature

At an art exhibition recently, I saw a painting that had sold for $5,000. The artist was a young nobody from the West named Kraft, who had a favorite meal and a cherished belief. His sustenance was an unwavering faith in the Perfect Artistic Balance of Nature. His theory revolved around corned beef hash topped with a poached egg. There was a story behind that painting, so I went home and let it flow from my pen. Kraft's concept—but that's not where the story begins.

Three years ago, Kraft, Bill Judkins (a poet), and I ate our meals at Cypher's restaurant on Eighth Avenue. I say "ate." When we had money, Cypher would take it "off of" us, as he put it. We had no credit arrangement; we would go in, order food and eat it. We either paid or we didn't pay. We trusted in Cypher's grumpiness and simmering anger. Deep down in his gloomy soul he was either a prince, a fool, or an artist. He sat at a termite-damaged desk, piled high with stacks of waiters' checks so old that I was convinced the one at the very bottom was for clams that Henry Hudson had eaten and paid for. Cypher possessed the ability, shared with Napoleon III and the bulging-eyed perch, of casting a veil over his eyes, making the windows of his soul cloudy and unreadable. Once when we left him unpaid, offering ridiculous excuses, I glanced back and saw him trembling with silent laughter behind his veil. From time to time we would settle our old debts.

But the most important thing at Cypher's was Milly. Milly worked as a waitress. She was a perfect example of Kraft's theory about the artistic adjustment of nature. She

17

belonged, in large part, to the art of serving tables, just as Minerva belonged to the art of fighting, or Venus to the science of serious romance. If she had been placed on a pedestal and cast in bronze, she could have stood alongside the greatest of her heroic sisters as "Liver-and-Bacon Bringing Life to the World." She was part of Cypher's. You expected to see her enormous figure emerge through that thick blue cloud of smoke from frying grease just as you expect the Palisades to appear through drifting fog over the Hudson River. There, surrounded by the steam from vegetables and the vapors from endless plates of "ham and eggs," the crash of dishes, the clatter of metal utensils, the shouting of "quick orders," the calls of hungry customers and all the terrible noise of feeding people, surrounded by swarms of buzzing winged creatures left to us by Pharaoh, Milly navigated her magnificent path like some great ocean liner cutting through the canoes of screaming savages.

Our Goddess of Food was built with such magnificent proportions that you could only look at her with wonder. Her sleeves were always rolled up past her elbows. She could have picked up all three of us friends in her hands and tossed us right out the window. She was younger than any of us, but she possessed such magnificent womanhood and natural grace that she took care of us like a mother from day one. She served us Cypher's food supplies with royal disregard for cost and amount, as if pouring from an endless horn of plenty that never ran dry. Her voice rang out like a massive silver bell; her smile showed many teeth and appeared constantly; she seemed like a golden sunrise over mountain peaks. I never looked at her without thinking of Yosemite. And yet, somehow, I could never imagine her existing anywhere outside of Cypher's. Nature had positioned her there, and she had planted herself and flourished tremendously. She appeared content, and collected her meager wages on Saturday nights with the excited joy of a child receiving an unexpected gift.

It was Kraft who first expressed the fear that each of us must have been secretly harboring. The topic arose naturally, as it happened, from certain artistic questions we were debating. One of us drew a comparison between the harmony that exists between a Haydn symphony and pistachio ice cream to the perfect compatibility between Milly and Cypher's.

"There's a particular destiny looming over Milly," Kraft said, "and if it catches up with her, she'll be lost to Cypher's and to us."

"She will grow fat?" asked Judkins, fearfully.

"She's going to attend night school and become more refined?" I asked nervously.

"Here's the thing," said Kraft, emphasizing his point by jabbing his rigid finger into a puddle of spilled coffee. "Caesar had his Brutus—cotton has its bollworm, the chorus girl has her Pittsburgh millionaire, the summer vacationer has his poison ivy, the hero has his Carnegie medal, art has its Morgan, the rose has its—"

"Speak," I interrupted, deeply troubled. "You don't think that Milly will start drinking, do you?"

"One day," Kraft concluded solemnly, "a millionaire lumberman from Wisconsin will come to Cypher's for a plate of beans, and he will marry Milly."

"Never!" Judkins and I cried out in horror.

"A lumberman," Kraft repeated, his voice hoarse.

"And a millionaire lumberman!" I sighed in despair.

"From Wisconsin!" Judkins groaned.

We agreed that this terrible fate seemed to threaten her. Few things were more likely to happen. Milly, like some enormous untouched expanse of pine forest, was destined to attract the lumberman's attention. And we knew well the behavior of the Badgers once luck favored them. They head straight to New York and offer everything they have to the girl who serves them food in a cheap restaurant. Why, even the alphabet itself seems to conspire. The Sunday newspaper headline writer's job is already done for him.

"Charming Waitress Marries Rich Wisconsin Lumberjack."

For a while we felt that Milly was on the verge of being lost to us.

It was our love of Nature's Perfect Artistic Balance that motivated us. We couldn't hand her over to a lumber baron, doubly cursed by money and narrow-mindedness. We cringed at the thought of Milly, with her voice refined and her elbows properly covered, serving tea in the marble mansion of someone who destroys trees. Never! She belonged at Cypher's—surrounded by the smell of bacon grease, the aroma of boiled cabbage, and the magnificent, operatic symphony of crashing heavy dishes and clattering serving carts.

Our fears must have turned out to be prophetic, because that very evening the wilderness sent us Milly's destined captor—the price we had to pay for balance and order. But Alaska, not Wisconsin, would bear the weight of this reckoning.

We were eating our dinner of beef stew and dried apples when he hurried in as if following behind a dog sled team, and joined our group at the table. With the casual openness typical of camp life, he bombarded us with conversation and sought the companionship of men stranded in the wilderness of a cheap restaurant. We welcomed him as an interesting character, and within three minutes we had nearly become lifelong friends ready to die for each other.

He was rough-looking with a beard and weathered by the wind. He mentioned that he had just finished traveling the "trail" and arrived at one of the North River ferries. I imagined I could still see the snow dust from Chilcoot covering his shoulders. Then he scattered nuggets, stuffed ptarmigans, beadwork, and seal pelts across the table—the typical treasures of a returning Klondiker—and started boasting to us about his millions.

"Bank drafts worth two million dollars," he concluded, "plus a thousand dollars a day accumulating from my mining claims. Now I'd like some beef stew and canned peaches. I haven't left the train since I departed from Seattle, and I'm starving. The food the porters serve on Pullman cars doesn't satisfy me. You gentlemen can order whatever you'd like."

And then Milly appeared with countless dishes balanced on her bare arm—she loomed large and pale and rosy and magnificent like Mount Saint Elias—wearing a smile that was like dawn breaking in a canyon. The Klondiker dropped his furs and gold nuggets as if they were worthless, his mouth fell open halfway, and he gazed at her in amazement. You could practically see the diamond crowns he imagined placing on Milly's head and the hand-stitched silk Parisian gowns he planned to purchase for her.

At last the bollworm had attacked the cotton—the poison ivy was stretching out its tendrils to wrap around the summer visitor—the millionaire lumber baron, barely disguised as an Alaskan prospector, was about to swallow up our Milly and disrupt Nature's balance.

Kraft was the first to move. He jumped up and slapped the Klondiker's back. "Come out and have a drink," he yelled. "Drink first and eat later." Judkins grabbed one arm while I took the other. Cheerfully, loudly, and with unstoppable energy, in true good-fellow fashion, we pulled him from the restaurant to a bar, cramming his pockets with his preserved birds and tough-to-chew nuggets.

There he grumbled a somewhat good-natured objection. "That's the woman I want," he announced. "She can share my meals for the rest of her life. I've never seen such a wonderful girl. I'm going back there to ask her to marry me. I bet she won't want to work as a waitress anymore when she sees how much money I've got."

"You'll have another whiskey and milk now," Kraft urged, with a devilish grin. "I thought you guys from the countryside had more backbone."

Kraft used up his small amount of money at the bar and then looked at Judkins and me with such a pleading expression that we spent every last cent we had buying drinks for our guest.

When our ammunition ran out and the Klondiker, still relatively sober, started rambling about Milly again, Kraft whispered a courteous yet cutting insult in his ear about people who were stingy with their money. This caused the miner to slam down handful after handful of silver coins and bills, demanding every drink imaginable to wash away the accusation.

The task was completed. We used his own weapons to force him off the battlefield. Afterward, we had him transported to a remote small hotel where he was placed in bed, surrounded by his gold nuggets and baby seal pelts.

"He'll never find Cypher's again," Kraft said. "He'll propose to the first white apron he sees in a dairy restaurant tomorrow. And Milly—I mean the Natural Adjustment—is saved!"

And back to Cypher's the three of us went, and finding few customers there, we joined hands and performed an Indian dance with Milly in the center.

This happened three years ago. Around that same time, a bit of good fortune came our way, and the three of us were able to afford more expensive and less healthy food than what Cypher offered. Our lives went in different directions, and I never saw Kraft again and rarely encountered Judkins.

But, as I mentioned, I recently saw a painting that sold for $5,000. It was titled "Boadicea," and the figure appeared to dominate the entire outdoor landscape. However, among all the admirers gathered in front of it, I think I was the only one who wished Boadicea would step out of her frame and bring me corned-beef hash with a poached egg.

I rushed off to visit Kraft. His devilish eyes remained unchanged, his hair was even more disheveled, but his clothing had been crafted by a professional tailor.

"I didn't know," I said to him.

"We bought a cottage in the Bronx with the money," he said. "Any evening at 7."

"Then," I said, "when you led us against the lumberman—the—Klondiker—it wasn't entirely because of the Unerring Artistic Adjustment of Nature?"

"Well, not entirely," said Kraft, with a grin.

THE END

Thank You For Reading

You've Just Read a Piece of the Greatest Library Ever Rebuilt

Thank you for reading.

This book is one of thousands we're restoring, reimagining, and translating as part of the **Modern Library of Alexandria** — a global movement to preserve and share humanity's most important ideas.

What was once lost to fire and time is now rising again — not just as memory, but as living, breathing knowledge, freely accessible to all.

What You Can Do Next:

- **Keep Reading.**

  Discover more legendary works — in beautiful print, audiobook, or digital form — at LibraryofAlexandria.com.

- **Build Your Own Library.**

  Every title is available as a paperback, hardcover, or collectible boxset — at true printing cost. Craft a personal library worthy of display.

- **Spread the Light.**

  Share this book. Tell others about the movement. Help us translate every timeless work into every language, so no reader is ever left behind.

By finishing this book, you've already taken part in something extraordinary.

Join us at LibraryofAlexandria.com

Together, we're rebuilding the greatest library the world has ever known.

With appreciation,

The Modern Library of Alexandria Team

Visit:
www.libraryofalexandria.com
Or scan the code below: